THE INDIAN ARCHITECTURE

AN EXPLORATION OF INDIAN TEMPLE, PALACE, AND MONUMENTAL ARCHITECTURE

DR. JAGADEESH PILLAI

|| "Dedicated to all who seek to understand and appreciate Indian culture and tradition." ||

Contents

Contents

Prayer

"Om Poornamadah Poornamidam Poornat Poornamudachyate,Poornasya Poornamaadaya Poornamevavashishyate,Om Shantih, Shantih, Shantih"

The literal interpretation of this mantra is: That which is Absolute, This which is Absolute, Absolute arises from Absolute, If Absolute is removed from Absolute, Absolute remains OM Peace, Peace, Peace.

ᐧᐧᐧ

About The Author

Dr. Jagadeesh Pillai is a renowned Guinness World Record holder, writer, and researcher hailing from Varanasi, also known as the abode of Lord Shiva. With a Ph.D. in Vedic Science and a range of creative ideas and achievements, he is a true polymath. He is the author of more than 100 books including Research Publications. Although his roots can be traced back to Kerala, the people of Varanasi hold him in high regard and affectionately consider him one of their own.

Dr. Pillai has achieved four Guinness World Records in the following subjects:

"Script to Screen" - In this record, Dr. Pillai produced and directed an animation film within the shortest time possible, breaking the previous record set by Canadians. He has also received numerous national and international awards and recognitions for this achievement.

Longest Line of Postcards - For this record, Dr. Pillai created a line of 16,300 postcards on the occasion of the 163rd anniversary of Indian Postal Day. The event also included a questionnaire about the Indian flag.

Largest Poster Awareness Campaign - Dr. Pillai designed an awareness campaign on the subject of "Beti Bachao - Beti Padhao" (Save the Girl Child - Educate the Girl Child) to achieve this record.

Largest Envelope - In tribute to the Indian Prime Minister's

"Make in India" initiative, Dr. Pillai created a 4000 square meter envelope using waste paper to achieve this record.

Attempted - **70000 Candles on a 210 kg Cake** - To celebrate the 70th Indian Independence Day, Dr. Pillai attempted to light 70,000 candles on a 210 kg cake, which was recorded in World Records India.

Attempted - **Documentary on Dhamek Stupa of Sarnath in 17 Languages** - Dr. Pillai attempted to create a documentary on the Dhamek Stupa of Sarnath, dubbing it in 17 different languages. The result of this attempt is currently awaiting confirmation from the Guinness World Records.

Dr. Pillai is skilled in teaching the Bhagavad Gita, a Hindu scripture, and is popular among young people. He has helped many young people improve their lives through his motivational teachings.

In addition to teaching, he has composed and sung numerous Sanskrit Bhajans and patriotic songs.

He has also written and directed several short films and documentaries for awareness campaigns, and has volunteered with the police in both UP and Kerala to spread awareness about various issues through videos and photography.

Incredibly, he has produced and directed over 100 documentaries about the city of Varanasi, all on his own.

He has also helped and guided more than 25 boys and girls to achieve world records through creative and innovative methods. He is a multifaceted person who uses his intellect and the blessings given to him by God to excel in various areas. He is both a teacher and a student, always learning and teaching, and is able to master any subject he comes across.

He is a selfless social activist and motivational speaker who has overcome struggles and failures to become a successful and enthusiastic individual with a rich life experience.

In addition to his work with the Bhagavad Gita, he is also an efficient Tarot card reader, Astro-Vastu consultant, and a talented singer and composer. He has sung the entire Ram Charita Manas and Bhagavad Gita in his own compositions, and has sung the phrase "Lokah Samastha Sukhino Bhavantu" in 50 different languages. He is currently working on a detailed and scientific study of Vedas, Upanishads, Puranas, and the Bhagavad Gita. He has also composed and sung the Hanuman Chalisa and Gayatri Mantra in 108 and 1008 different compositions, respectively.

Awards - Four Times Guinness World Records, Winner of Mahatma Gandhi Vishwa Shanti Puraskar, Mahatma Gandhi Global Peace Ambassador, Kashi Ratna Award, Dr. APJ Abdul Kalam Motivational Person of the Year 2017, Mother Teresa Award, Indira Gandhi Priyadarshini Award, Bharat Vikas Ratna Award, Udyog Ratna Award, Vigyan Prasar Award, Poorvanchal Ratn Samman.

ॐॐॐ

Preface

The Indian subcontinent is a land of architectural marvels, a testament to the skill and creativity of the architects, engineers, and builders of the past. From ancient Indus Valley Civilization to medieval temple architecture, Mughal palaces and British colonial buildings, the architecture of India reflects the country's rich cultural heritage and history.

This book, "The Indian Architecture: An Exploration of Indian Temple, Palace, and Monumental Architecture" is a comprehensive guide to the diverse and fascinating world of Indian architecture. The book delves into the evolution of Indian temple architecture, from the Indus Valley Civilization to the medieval period, and also explores the palace architecture of India from the Rajput to Mughal era. Additionally, the book covers the monumental architecture of India, from the iconic Taj Mahal to other famous monuments, and also discusses the South and North Indian temple architecture, their styles, and characteristics. The book also examines the Islamic, colonial, and contemporary architecture in India, and how it has influenced Indian architecture. The book concludes with an examination of the architecture of sustainability and preservation for future generations.

This book is written for anyone who is interested in Indian architecture, whether you are a student, an architect, a historian, or simply someone who is fascinated by the beauty and diversity of Indian architecture. It provides an in-depth look at the history, styles, and techniques of Indian architecture, and also examines the cultural, social, and political influences that have shaped the architecture of India.

We hope that this book will inspire you to look at Indian architecture with fresh eyes and to appreciate the skill, creativity, and cultural heritage of the architects, engineers and builders of the past and present.

ᗞᗞᗞ

ONE

THE EVOLUTION OF INDIAN TEMPLE ARCHITECTURE: FROM INDUS VALLEY CIVILIZATION TO MEDIEVAL PERIOD

The Indus Valley Civilization, which flourished in the northwestern region of the Indian subcontinent around 3300 BCE to 1300 BCE, is known for its advanced city planning, monumental architecture, and sophisticated engineering. However, there is no evidence of dedicated religious structures from this period, suggesting that the Indus Valley people may have practiced a form of animism rather than organized religion.

The earliest evidence of religious structures in India comes from the Vedic period, around 1500 BCE to 600 BCE, in the form of fire altars. These were simple structures used for performing sacrifices and were constructed of brick and timber.

As Hinduism developed and evolved, so did temple architecture. The Gupta period, between 320 CE and 550 CE, saw the development of the first stone temples, and during the Medieval period, between 600 CE and 1200 CE, temple architecture reached new heights with the construction of large, elaborate stone temples in the Nagara and Dravidian styles. These temples were characterized by their towering spires, intricately carved sculptures, and complex architectural plans.

During the medieval period, temple architecture also became more diverse with the development of different regional styles. For example, temples in the South Indian Dravidian style were characterized by their large pyramidal towers, while temples in the North Indian Nagara style had a curvilinear tower, known as a shikhara.

Temple architecture in India has undergone a significant evolution, from simple fire altars in the Vedic period, to large, elaborate stone temples in the medieval period.

ᏋᏋᏋ

"India is the mother of all civilizations. India is the fountain of the world's cultures. India is the seed-ground of the world's religions."
- Mahatma Gandhi

❦❦❦

TWO

PALACE ARCHITECTURE IN INDIA: FROM RAJPUT TO MUGHAL ERA

The Rajput era, which lasted from the 8th to the 18th century, saw the construction of many grand palaces and forts, such as the Amber Fort in Jaipur, the Chittorgarh Fort in Chittorgarh and the Mehrangarh Fort in Jodhpur. These palaces were built as symbols of power and prestige, and were characterized by their grand scale, intricate carvings, and decorative elements.

With the arrival of the Mughals in the 16th century, palace architecture in India began to change, as the Mughals brought with them new architectural styles and techniques from the Islamic world. Palaces such as the Agra Fort, the Red Fort in Delhi and the Jahangir Palace in Lahore, built during this time, were characterized by their fusion of Indian and Islamic architectural styles, with features such as large courtyards, ornate arches, and intricate tilework.

Mughal palaces also integrated elements of traditional Indian architecture, such as chhatris (small pavilions) and jalis (intricately carved screens), which added to the grandeur of the palaces. The Mughals also built a number of pleasure palaces, such as the Shish Mahal in the Lahore Fort, and the Khas Mahal in the Red Fort, which were used for leisure and entertainment.

Palace architecture in India has undergone a significant evolution, from the grand Rajput forts, built as symbols of power and prestige, to the Mughal palaces, which incorporated elements of traditional Indian architecture and Islamic architectural styles. The palaces built during these eras are not only architectural wonders but also historical landmarks, reflecting the culture, society and the political scenario of the time.

ppp

"India is the cradle of the human race, the birthplace of human speech, the mother of history, the grandmother of legend, and the great-grandmother of tradition."
- Mark Twain

ᕲᕲᕲ

THREE

MONUMENTAL ARCHITECTURE IN INDIA: THE TAJ MAHAL AND OTHER FAMOUS MONUMENTS

The Taj Mahal, located in Agra, is widely considered to be one of the most beautiful buildings in the world and is a UNESCO World Heritage site. It was built by Mughal Emperor Shah Jahan in memory of his wife Mumtaz Mahal, and construction began in 1632 and was completed in 1653. The Taj Mahal is an iconic example of Mughal architecture, a blend of Indian, Persian and Islamic architectural styles, and is known for its intricate carvings, inlaid marble work and stunning gardens.

Another famous monumental architecture in India is the Qutub Minar located in Delhi, which is the tallest brick minaret in the world. It was built in the 12th century by Qutub-ud-din Aibak, the first Muslim ruler of Delhi, and is an excellent example of the Indo-Islamic architectural style. The Qutub Minar complex also includes several other monuments, such as the Alai Darwaza and the Iron Pillar, which are also examples of the remarkable architectural skills of the time.

The Sun Temple in Konark, Odisha is another famous monumental architecture in India, built in the 13th century, it is an outstanding example of Kalinga architecture. The temple is shaped like a giant chariot, with twelve pairs of wheels, and it is richly decorated with sculptures of gods, goddesses and celestial musicians. The temple is a UNESCO World Heritage site and is known for its intricate carvings, and its architectural style, which reflects the skill of the Kalinga craftsmen.

India has a rich history of monumental architecture, and the Taj Mahal, Qutub Minar, and the Sun Temple are just a few examples of the country's architectural heritage. These monuments are not only architectural wonders, but also historical landmarks, reflecting the culture, society, and the political scenario of the time. They also showcase the skill and creativity of the architects, engineers, and craftsmen who built them and continue to inspire visitors from all over the world.

▷▷▷

"India is a land of ancient culture and
wisdom, and these are qualities that cannot
be easily bought or sold."
- Dalai Lama

ᗡᗡᗡ

FOUR

THE SOUTH INDIAN TEMPLE ARCHITECTURE: DRAVIDIAN STYLE AND ITS CHARACTERISTICS

The Dravidian style of temple architecture is known for its distinctive pyramidal towers, known as gopurams, which are typically built at the entrance of the temple. These towers are usually multi-tiered and decorated with intricate carvings of gods, goddesses, and mythological creatures. They also feature a kalasha, a bulbous structure at the top of the tower, which is considered to be a symbol of the cosmic axis.

Another characteristic of the Dravidian style is the use of multiple enclosures, or prakarams, around the main sanctum sanctorum. These enclosures typically have walls decorated with reliefs and sculptures and are used for circumambulation by devotees.

The Dravidian style also features a mandapa, a pillared hall, which serves as the main gathering space for devotees. These mandapas are usually open to the elements, and their pillars are often decorated with intricate carvings.

The Dravidian style of temple architecture is known for its emphasis on symmetry and proportion. The temples are typically built on a square or rectangular plan, and the layout is designed to create a sense of balance and harmony.

The Dravidian style of temple architecture is characterized by its distinctive pyramidal towers, multiple enclosures, and mandapas. The style is known for its emphasis on symmetry and proportion, and the intricate carvings, sculptures and reliefs that adorn the temples. The Dravidian style is not only a reflection of the religious and cultural influences of the time but also showcases the skill and creativity of the architects, engineers and craftsmen who built them. Some of the famous examples of Dravidian style temples are Meenakshi Temple, Sri Ranganathaswamy Temple and the Sri Brihadeeswarar Temple.

ﮒﮒﮒ

"The culture of India is the mother of all cultures, because it is old, because it sustains."
- Jiddu Krishnamurti

ᐅᐅᐅ

FIVE

THE NORTH INDIAN TEMPLE ARCHITECTURE: NAGARA STYLE AND ITS CHARACTERISTICS

The Nagara style of temple architecture is characterized by its distinctive curvilinear tower, known as a shikhara. The shikhara, which is typically built over the main sanctum of the temple, is often ornately decorated with intricate carvings, sculptures, and moldings. The shikhara is often divided into several storeys, each with its own distinct decoration.

Another characteristic of the Nagara style is the use of a

mandapa, a pillared hall, which serves as the main gathering space for devotees. These mandapas are usually open to the elements, and their pillars are often decorated with intricate carvings.

The Nagara style of temple architecture is also known for its emphasis on verticality, which is achieved through the use of a series of diminishing storeys, each with its own distinct decoration. The temples are typically built on a square or rectangular plan, and the layout is designed to create a sense of balance and harmony.

The North Indian temple architecture also has a rich tradition of using intricate sculptures and carvings, which are found on the walls and pillars of the temples, and in the niches and recesses of the shikhara. These sculptures and carvings depict various scenes from Hindu mythology and religious stories, as well as images of gods and goddesses.

The Nagara style of temple architecture is characterized by its distinctive curvilinear shikhara, mandapas, and emphasis on verticality. The style is known for its rich tradition of intricate sculptures and carvings, which adorn the temples and reflect the religious and cultural influences of the time. The Nagara style of temple architecture is also known for its emphasis on balance and harmony, and the skill and creativity of the architects, engineers, and craftsmen who built them. Some of the famous examples of Nagara style temples are Khajuraho temple, Somnath temple, and the Kandariya Mahadeva temple. These temples not only serve as a place of worship but also as an architectural marvels and a testimony to the rich cultural heritage of India.

DR. JAGADEESH PILLAI

❦❦❦

"The spiritual heritage of India is the most precious treasure that mankind possesses."
- Swami Vivekananda

ᐅᐅᐅ

SIX

Islamic Architecture in India: The influence of Islamic Architecture on Indian Architecture

Islamic architecture was introduced to India during the 12th century, with the arrival of the Sultanate period. This period saw the construction of many Islamic monuments and structures, such as the Qutub Minar in Delhi, the Alai

Darwaza in Delhi, and the Adhai Din Ka Jhonpra in Ajmer. These structures were characterized by their use of Islamic architectural elements such as arches, domes, and minarets, as well as intricate geometric patterns and calligraphy.

During the Mughal period, which lasted from the 16th to the 19th century, Islamic architecture had a profound influence on Indian architecture. Mughal emperors, such as Akbar, Jahangir and Shah Jahan, commissioned the construction of many grand palaces and monuments, such as the Agra Fort, the Red Fort in Delhi, and the Taj Mahal. These structures were characterized by their fusion of Indian and Islamic architectural styles, with features such as large courtyards, ornate arches, and intricate tilework.

The Islamic architecture also had an impact on the Indian domestic architecture, this is visible in the traditional Indian havelis, which are found in the northern regions of India. These havelis are characterized by their use of Islamic architectural elements such as arches, jalis and courtyards, which were incorporated into the traditional Indian architectural styles.

Islamic architecture has had a profound influence on Indian architecture, from the Sultanate period to the Mughal period, and even today. The Islamic architectural elements such as arches, domes, and minarets, as well as the intricate geometric patterns and calligraphy, have been adapted and incorporated into Indian architectural styles. These Islamic architectural influences not only reflect the historical and cultural exchange between the Islamic and Indian civilizations but also showcase the skill and creativity of the architects, engineers and craftsmen who built them.

"India is the land of spirituality, and the spiritual teachings of India have been a source of inspiration for the entire world."
- Sri Sri Ravi Shankar

SEVEN

Colonial Architecture in India: The Impact of British Colonialism on Indian Architecture

During the British colonial period, which lasted from the 18th to the 20th century, British architects and engineers introduced new architectural styles and techniques to India. The British, who were influenced by the neoclassical and gothic styles of architecture, built many grand public buildings, such as government buildings, courts, and churches, in these styles.

One of the most notable examples of colonial architecture in India is the Victoria Memorial in Kolkata, which was built in the late 19th century in the neoclassical style. This grand marble building, which serves as a museum and art gallery, was built to commemorate the reign of Queen Victoria and is a fine example of British colonial architecture in India.

British colonial architecture also had a significant impact on the residential architecture in India. They introduced new building techniques, such as load-bearing brickwork, and styles, such as the Georgian and Victorian styles, which were used to construct many homes and bungalows for the British officials and upper-class Indians.

In addition to the impact on building styles, British colonialism also had an impact on the urban planning and development of Indian cities. Many British colonial cities, such as Mumbai, Kolkata, and Chennai, were designed with grid-like street patterns, large public spaces, and grand public buildings. This urban planning, which was heavily influenced by the European models, left a lasting impact on the cities in India.

British colonialism had a significant impact on the architecture of India. The British introduced new architectural styles and techniques, such as neoclassical and gothic styles, and the introduction of the load-bearing brickwork. These new styles and techniques were used to construct grand public buildings, homes and bungalows, and had an impact on the urban planning of Indian cities. The colonial architecture in India not only reflects the historical and cultural exchange between the British and Indian civilizations but also showcases the skill and creativity of the architects, engineers, and builders of that time.

ÞÞÞ

"India is the one country in the world where spiritualism and science are not in conflict." - Dr. APJ Abdul Kalam

⊳⊳⊳

EIGHT

CONTEMPORARY INDIAN ARCHITECTURE: THE MODERN ERA AND ITS IMPACT

The modern era of architecture in India can be traced back to the independence of India in 1947, when the country began to establish its own architectural identity. The early years of the modern era saw the emergence of architects such as Charles Correa and Raj Rewal, who were heavily influenced by the International Style of architecture. They began to design buildings that reflected the Indian culture, climate, and context, but also incorporated modern materials and construction techniques.

One of the most notable examples of contemporary Indian

architecture is the Indian Institute of Technology, Kanpur (IITK) designed by Charles Correa. The IITK is considered to be one of the most important buildings of the modern era in India and is an excellent example of how contemporary Indian architecture can reflect the Indian culture, climate, and context.

In recent years, contemporary Indian architecture has continued to evolve, with architects experimenting with new materials, construction techniques, and technologies. This has led to the emergence of new architectural styles, such as sustainable architecture, which seeks to minimize the environmental impact of buildings while maximizing energy efficiency.

Contemporary Indian architecture also reflects the rapid urbanization and modernization of the country, with architects designing buildings that are not only functional and sustainable but also aesthetically pleasing. Many new buildings are now being built in Indian cities, such as Mumbai and New Delhi, that reflect the latest trends in international architecture, while also incorporating traditional Indian architectural elements.

Contemporary Indian architecture reflects the country's unique culture, climate, and context, while also incorporating modern materials, construction techniques, and technologies. The modern era of architecture in India has led to the emergence of new architectural styles, such as sustainable architecture, and has had a significant impact on the built environment of the country. Contemporary Indian architecture continues to evolve, reflecting the rapid urbanization and modernization of India, and the skill and creativity of the architects, engineers and builders of the modern era.

ÞÞÞ

• 37 •

"The culture of India is a rich mixture of
tradition, spirituality, and modernity."
- Ratan Tata

▷▷▷

NINE

The Architecture of Sustainability: Indian Traditional Architecture and its Impact on Modern Sustainable Architecture

Traditional Indian architecture has always been closely tied to the natural environment, with architects and builders using locally sourced materials, construction techniques and designs that respond to the local climate, and promote energy efficiency. For example, Indian traditional architecture often includes features such as courtyards, which provide natural ventilation and light, and verandahs which provide shade and protection from the sun.

In recent years, architects and builders have been looking to traditional Indian architecture for inspiration and guidance in the development of sustainable buildings. Many modern sustainable buildings in India now incorporate traditional architectural elements such as courtyards and verandahs, as well as traditional construction techniques, such as mud and bamboo construction, which are not only sustainable but also cost-effective.

One example of a contemporary building that draws inspiration from traditional Indian architecture is the Indian Habitat Centre in New Delhi. Designed by architect Raj Rewal, the building incorporates traditional Indian architectural elements such as courtyards and verandahs, as well as modern sustainable features such as solar panels and rainwater harvesting.

In addition to the incorporation of traditional architectural elements, many architects and builders in India are also looking to traditional Indian building practices, such as

Vastu Shastra and Sthapatya Veda, which are ancient Indian texts that provide guidelines for designing and building structures that are in harmony with nature.

Indian traditional architecture has had a significant impact on the development of sustainable architecture in modern India. Many contemporary sustainable buildings in India now incorporate traditional architectural elements and building practices, which promote energy efficiency, reduce environmental impact and also reflect the local culture, climate and context. Traditional Indian architecture not only provides inspiration for sustainable design but also showcases the skill and creativity of the architects, engineers, and builders of the past, and continues to be a source of inspiration for the future.

 PPP

"The spiritual richness of India is a result of the deep understanding of the human mind and the possibilities of its transformation."
- Jiddu Krishnamurti

ᐅᐅᐅ

TEN

THE ARCHITECTURE OF LEISURE: INDIAN GARDENS, PARKS, AND RECREATIONAL SPACES

Indian gardens and parks have a long history, dating back to ancient times, when they were used for meditation, recreation, and as a symbol of wealth and power. Many traditional Indian gardens, such as the Mughal gardens, are known for their intricate geometric designs, which often incorporate water features such as fountains and ponds, as well as a variety of plants and trees.

One of the most famous examples of Indian gardens is the Taj Mahal, which was built in the 17th century by the Mughal emperor Shah Jahan as a symbol of his love for his wife. The gardens of the Taj Mahal are known for their symmetrical design, which incorporates water features and a variety of plants and trees.

In addition to traditional gardens, contemporary Indian architects and builders have also been designing and constructing modern gardens, parks, and recreational spaces that reflect the Indian culture and context. Many of these spaces incorporate traditional Indian architectural elements, such as water features, as well as modern amenities such as playgrounds and sports facilities.

In recent years, there has been a growing interest in sustainable landscape design in India, with architects and builders designing gardens, parks, and recreational spaces that are not only visually pleasing but also ecologically sustainable. Many of these spaces incorporate features such as rainwater harvesting, solar power, and the use of native plants and trees.

Indian gardens, parks, and recreational spaces reflect the country's rich cultural heritage and provide a space for leisure, recreation, and reflection. The traditional Indian gardens and parks are known for their intricate geometric designs and water features, while contemporary gardens, parks, and recreational spaces incorporate traditional elements as well as modern amenities and sustainable features. These spaces not only showcase the skill and creativity of the architects, engineers, and builders of the past and present but also reflect the cultural and ecological context of India.

❦❦❦

"India's culture is the mother of all cultures, beaming with confidence, faith, and spiritual depth."

- Ratan Tata

The Living Heritage: Indian Architecture and its Preservation for Future Generations

India has a rich architectural heritage, which includes a wide variety of buildings, from ancient Indus Valley Civilization to medieval temple architecture and British colonial architecture. This heritage is not only a reflection of the country's history and culture, but also an important part of its identity.

However, many of these buildings are facing threats such as urbanization, neglect, and lack of maintenance. In recent years, there has been a growing awareness of the importance of preserving Indian architecture for future generations.

The government of India has established various organizations and initiatives to preserve and protect the country's architectural heritage. The Archaeological Survey of India (ASI) is the primary agency responsible for the conservation of ancient monuments and archaeological sites in India. The ASI works to preserve and protect the country's architectural heritage by carrying out conservation and restoration work, as well as by providing technical assistance to other organizations and individuals.

In addition to government efforts, there are also various non-governmental organizations and private individuals who are working to preserve Indian architecture. These organizations and individuals often work to raise awareness about the importance of preserving Indian architecture and to advocate for the conservation and restoration of specific buildings and sites.

In recent years, there has been a growing interest in sustainable preservation, this approach aims to conserve the architectural heritage while also addressing the needs of the present and future generations. This is done by incorporating sustainable technologies, materials and methods to preserve the heritage buildings, and also by promoting public awareness and participation in the preservation process.

Indian architecture is a living heritage that reflects the country's history and culture. There is a growing awareness and efforts by the government, non-governmental organizations and private individuals to preserve and protect this heritage for future generations. These efforts include conservation, restoration, and sustainable preservation, which not only maintain the architectural heritage but also promote public awareness and participation in the preservation process. The preservation of Indian architecture is not just a matter of preserving the buildings but also preserving a part of the country's cultural heritage and identity.

ᗐᗐᗐ

Other Books Of The Author

30. Rigveda in a Nutshell
31. Yajurveda in a Nutshell
32. Samveda in a Nutshell
33. Atharva Veda in a Nutshell
34. Ayushman Bhava - Ayurveda
35. Srimad Bhagavad Gita and Upanishad Connection
36. Srimad Bhagavad Gita - an attempt to summarize each chapter.
37. Facts and Impact of Nakshatra
38. Astro Gems - NAVARATNA
39. Ekadashi - A Concise Overview
40. A Concise View of Hanuman Chalisa
41. Inspirational Gita
42. Nakshatraranyam
43. Summary of 18 Mahapuranas
44. Synopsis of 18 Upa Puranas
45. Rigvediya Upanishads
46. Shukla Yajurvediya Upanishads
47. Krishna Yajurvediya Upanishads
48. Samavediya Upanishads
49. Atharvavediya Upanishads
50. The Seven Great Sages
51. From Rocket Scientist to President Dr. APJ Abdul Kalam
52. The Visionary's Voice - Quotes of Dr. APJ Abdul Kalam
53. The Wisdom of Swami Vivekananda: Insights and Inspiration from a Legendary Spiritual Teacher
54. Ayurvedic Remedies from the Garden
55. Sages and Seers
56. Rising Strong – Motivational Stories of Women
57. Beyond Flames -Mystery stories of Funeral Ghat Manikarnika
58. The Origins of Tulsi: A Look at the Mythological Roots of the Plant"

ﻙﻙﻙ

Contact

DR. JAGADEESH PILLAI

PhD in Vedic Science

Four Times Guinness World Record Holder

Winner of Mahatma Gandhi Vishwa Shanti Puraskar and
Global Peace Ambassador

Gemology, Astro & Vastu Consultant - Spiritual Counselor

Consultant for designing World Record Ideas

Efficient Tarot Card Reader

9839093003

myrichindia@gmail.com

drjagadeeshpillai@facebook

drjagadeeshpillai@instagram

jagadeeshpillai@youtube

www. JAGADEESHPILLAI.com

❦❦❦

|| LOKAHA SAMASTHAHA SUKHINO BHAVANTU ||

• 63 •